Healthy & Tasty:
Dr. J's Anti-Yeast Cooking

By Dr. Juliet Tien
D. N. Sc., M. S. N., B. S. N., R. N., C. S.

Infinite Success International
Publishing House
Las Vegas, Nevada

Library of Congress Catalog Card Number: 97-93150

ISBN: 1-890421-02-2

Printed in the United States of America

Dedication

This book is dedicated to my mother, who has taught me how to cook since I was six years old. It is also dedicated to my clients, who have enjoyed and appreciated my frozen anti-yeast vegetarian cuisine since 1989, and urged the birth of this book!

Preface

This cookbook is not meant to give you an extensive list of recipes. Rather, it teaches you basic principles of anti-yeast cooking. Once you are familiar with these principles, you will be able to create recipes to suit your taste.

When you create your own recipes, just remember to avoid using heavy spices. Heavy spices, such as spicy-hot red, green or black pepper, are too stimulating to your digestive tract and may cause diarrhea or heartburn if your digestive system is weak. Continuous and excessive use of heavy spices can also weaken the functioning of your liver and kidneys.

If you like garlic, feel free to add it to your lunch and dinner dishes. Fresh garlic is rich in vitamin C and good for your immune system. If you like cheese, you may use tofu cheese as a substitute. All the ingredients and cooking utensils can be purchased in health food stores, oriental grocery stores and most supermarkets.

Once you get used to my way of cooking and eating, you may not want to go back to the old way! Gook luck on your new journey and enjoy it!

Acknowledgments

To my daughter, Melisa Tien,
> an English major at UCLA who edited part of this book during her holiday break.

To my son, Charles Tien, an accounting major at USC,
> who edited part of this book and provided invaluable support to make the completion of this book possible.

To my mother, Chou-Chi Lee,
> who gave much help with housework which enabled me to finish this book within the least possible time.

To my friend, Roger Lindmark,
> who encouraged me to achieve my highest goals.

To my friend, Urbara Scott,
> who provided valuable editorial comments and showed much faith in me and my work.

To Bruni Pelletier,
> who meticulously proofread this book and loyally met deadlines.

To my clients,
> who shared invaluable feedback on my frozen anti-yeast nutritional cuisine in the past eight years, which led to the idea of publishing this book.

Table of Contents

Part I: Introduction 11

Part II: A Typical Day's Menu 21

Breakfast
Morning Snack
Lunch
Afternoon Snack
Dinner

Part III: Breakfast 25

Brown Rice or Oat Bran Cereal
Brown Rice Gruel
Oatmeal or Millet
Rye Toast

Part IV: Lunch and Dinner 31

Baked Potatoes or Yams
Brown Rice
Brown Rice Medley
Curried Potatoes
Egg Foo Yong
Ginger-Onion-Garlic Chicken
Ginger-Onion Fish

Grilled Tofu
Oriental Salad
Rice Noodle Delight
Steamed Fish
Steamed Vegetables
Stir-Fried Vegetables
Tofu Supreme

Part V: Sandwiches 47

Avocado Sandwich
Lentil Sandwich
Salmon Sandwich
Tofu Supreme Sandwich

Part VI: Soups 53

Barley Soup
Cauliflower Soup
Lentil Soup
Rice Noodle Soup
Split Pea Soup
Tofu-Seaweed Soup
Vegetable Soup
White Radish Soup

Part VII: Desserts 65

Brownies
Banana Ice Cream
Green Bean Soup
Oat Bran Cookies
Oat Bran Muffins
Red Bean Soup

Part VIII: Beverages 73

Caffeine-Free Herbal Tea
Rice Milk
Soy Milk
Unsweetened Apple Juice
Vegetable Juices
Other Beverages

Part IX: Frequently Asked Questions (FAQs) about Dr. J's Anti-Yeast Nutritional Program ..79

Part X: About the Author 83

Order Forms 91

Part I

Introduction

Many Americans are on diets to lose weight. "Diet" has thus become a dirty word to a lot of people. Diet denotes a restriction on variety, quantity and calories. What I am going to introduce to you in this book is not that kind of diet. Therefore, I prefer to call it a nutritional program.

> **This is a nutritional program you can follow for life that allows you to enjoy the foods you eat. This nutritional program feeds your body with essential nutrients to build your immunity, energy, mental clarity and productivity. I call this program an anti-yeast nutritional program, because it is also designed to control the yeast overgrowth in your body.**

Some of you may have read about other authors' anti-yeast nutritional programs and felt like it's a jungle out there. You may have found that different nutritionists have different opinions about what an anti-yeast or candida-free diet should consist of. Many of them conflict with each other. What you are about to learn here is not based on any theories; instead, it is based on my lifelong experience conquering yeast disorders and counseling thousands of people to achieve the same. If you have not read my book, ***Breaking the Yeast Curse: Food and Unconditional Love for Magic Healing,*** I urge you to do so. After you read the book, you will have a better understanding in terms of where I am coming from. To differentiate my nutritional program from others, let's call it ***Dr. J's anti-yeast nutritional program.***

In Dr. J's anti-yeast nutritional program, there are "Eight Commandments":

The Eight Commandments

of Dr. J's Anti-Yeast Nutritional Program

NO SUGAR

NO DAIRY

NO WHEAT

NO YEAST

NO ALCOHOL

NO CAFFEINE

NO NICOTINE

NO CHEMICALS

Some of my clients call me a "saint," because they are amazed by my discipline in following these "Eight Commandments." Once you learn how to find substitutes for the Standard American Diet (SAD), you can easily become a "saint," too! When you feel good after following Dr. J's anti-yeast nutritional program you will want to continue on the right track, being in the right state of mind.

Basically, this is a vegetarian cookbook. For people who have to take some time to wean themselves from animal protein, I included a few dishes of chicken and fish. Once you get used to being a "good vegetarian," meaning you know how to balance your protein, carbohydrate and fat intake, you will have a hard time eating meat again!

Dr. J's anti-yeast nutritional program contains more than 40% complex carbohydrates, less than 20% fat and less than 20% protein. This is in line with the American Heart Association's guidelines. What has gotten Americans in trouble is too much fat and too much protein. Some people are even thin on the outside but fat on the inside because of this excess fat and protein in the diet. They might have a trim appearance, but their blood vessels are clogged with fat.

It is a myth that you should not have any fat or salt. Good fat can facilitate the metabolism of bad fat. Your body needs good, dense fat to pad your organs and secure them at the right place. If you don't have the yellowish, dense fat in your body, you may suffer from an "organ dislocation" when you have an accident. In Dr. J's anti-yeast nutritional program, you will use a moderate amount of mono-unsaturated fat such as canola or olive oil for cooking. This will provide you with less than 20% fat you need to sustain a healthy body function.

You also need certain amount of salt in your body. Normal saline solution used for intravenous injections contains 0.9% of salt which is the closest to the salt concentration in your body fluids. Small amounts of sea salt are used in Dr. J's anti-yeast cooking to provide you with the balance of minerals and electrolytes.

Dr. J's anti-yeast nutritional program is for nourishing, not starving your body. In a typical day, you will take in at least 1,400 calories. Some people will cry out loud when they hear this. "I cannot even lose weight on so and so's program and they offer me 850 calories. If I could not lose weight on that amount of calories, how can I possibly lose weight on your 1,400 calorie program?" The answer is very simple. When your body is nourished by the right kind of food, your body will automatically shed unwanted fat. Fourteen hundred is the magic number! This will provide your body with the necessary calories to metabolize your fat. Any diet of less than 1,400 calories is a starvation diet. Starvation diets never work!

When you are on a starvation diet, in order for your body to preserve the ability to survive, your body will reach a point called "set point." Once your body gets used to this "set point," when you get off the starvation diet and get back on the Standard American Diet (which can be easily over 2,000 calories in one day, or even one meal), you quickly accumulate excess calories by leaps and bounds. That's why people gain much more weight back than what they lost in a very short period of time after they are off the starvation diet. Unfortunately, many Americans still have the quick-fix mentality and many business sectors take advantage of this mentality by offering a starvation diet or drugs!

Dr. J's anti-yeast nutritional program is not just designed for people to reduce weight. It is also designed for underweight people to gain weight. You can gain weight on the healthy food if you eat a large quantity. For those who are underweight, chances are you don't even consume more than 1,400 calories a day.

> **It is not necessary that you get into the habit of counting calories when you are on Dr. J's anti-yeast nutritional program. In fact, I don't want you to! The purpose of this cookbook is for you to learn how to feed your body based on natural rhythms.**

Your body is often smarter than you are. It tells you what is the right kind of foods and what is the right amount to eat. Unfortunately, you don't always listen to your body. Even though you have allergic reactions to some foods you still continue to eat them; or even though you are stuffed, you still continue to eat until your stomach feels heavy!

The Chinese have wisdom in portion control. A healthy eating habit is that you should not eat more than a handful of food for each meal. For those of you who love to eat, I bet you wish you had a bigger hand right now! A rule of thumb for Chinese is that you should stop eating when you are 80% full. There is a scientific basis for this ancient wisdom. It normally takes about 15 minutes for your stomach to send a message to your brain indicating that it's full; your brain then sends you a stop-eating command. If you wait until you receive this command to stop eating, you actually have overeaten by 15 minutes! Can you imagine how many calories you will have stored away in that 15 minutes of overeating, day in and day out?

Another reminder is no mushrooms, tomatoes nor eggplant. You can have anything else in the vegetable category. Review the book, ***Breaking the Yeast Curse: Food and Unconditional Love for Magic Healing*** to understand why. Always wash your vegetables or legumes very well in purified water before cooking. It goes without saying that you should use purified water for cooking. Always cook fresh foods; no canned foods.

The cooking utensils should be stainless steel, glass, ceramic, wood or bamboo. Avoid aluminum and iron; these can create chronic heavy metal poisoning. For stir-fry dishes, a wok on a gas stove will yield better results, because it makes it easier to control the amount of heat.

Don't leave leftover food in your refrigerator for more than two or three days; otherwise, they mildew, even though you might not be able to see it with your bare eyes. If you don't have time to prepare meals every day, you may cook a larger portion when you have time to cook. Save food in small containers and put them in the freezer. The extremely low temperature will not allow yeasts to grow. However, don't freeze your food for too long; otherwise, it loses its nutritional value. Also, a freezer which does not function well may cause spoilage after a few weeks. For a home freezer, don't store your food for more than two weeks.

If you want to take lunch with you to work, a good way to do it is prepare an extra portion in the evening when you fix supper. Put that extra meal in a plastic container and refrigerate it. If you have a microwave oven at work, less than five minutes of heating usually will not alter the nutritional value of the food. Only use microwave ovens to heat food, not to cook it. For those who do not like to use the microwave oven, you may heat your food on the stove. If you don't have a stove or microwave oven at work, here is a solution. Heat up your food on the stove in the morning before you go to work. Seal the heated food in a plastic container and wrap it in a plastic bag and a sandwich bag. By the time the lunch hour comes, your food is still lukewarm and does not lose its taste. Better yet, if you can find a thermos for carrying your lunch, you can enjoy a hot lunch without a stove or microwave oven at work! When there is a will, there is a way. Be creative!

The last principle to remember is to have frequent small meals rather than one or two large meals a day. A typical routine is to have three meals and two snacks (midmorning and midafternoon) a day. This routine will maintain your blood sugar at a steady level and prevent hypoglycemia. Many people skip the breakfast for the reason that they are not hungry in the morning. This is the worst thing that they can do to mess up their metabolic function.

> **Even if you are not hungry when you wake up, you need to eat a small breakfast to "wake up" and "train" your metabolic function! Otherwise, by the time your lunch hour comes you may feel so hungry that you want to eat a cow! This, in turn, can result in overeating!**

Now that we have covered all the bases, let's go ahead and get into the kitchen!

"A journey of a thousand miles begins with the first step." Take your first step toward healthier eating, no matter how hard it is. Each following step will become easier and easier!

Part II

A Typical Day's Menu

A sound mind in a sound body, is a short but full description of a happy state in this world.

John Locke
Some Thoughts Concerning Education, 1693

A Typical Day's Menu

Breakfast
1. Cooked oatmeal
2. A glass of rice milk or soy milk (preferably warm)
3. A few slices of banana
4. A sprinkle of pre-roasted slivered or sliced almonds
5. A sprinkle of unsweetened carob chips

Morning Snack
An oat bran cookie with a cup of caffeine-free herbal tea about two hours before lunch.

Lunch
1. One-half cup of short grain brown rice
2. One-half cup of slightly cooked vegetables (stir-fried or steamed)
3. One-half cup of tofu (any tofu dishes)
4. One cup of herbal tea (preferably warm)

Afternoon Snack
Fruit (e.g., a banana, an apple, a pear or a slice of ripe papaya)

Dinner
1. One-half cup of short grain brown rice
2. One-half cup of slightly cooked vegetables (stir-fried or steamed)
3. One-half cup of beans or tofu
4. One cup of soup

Please note:
The above menu will offer you approximately 1,400 calories; ideal for those of you who want to maintain ideal weight or reduce weight. For those of you who want to gain weight, just increase the portion of each item as desired.

Part III

Breakfast

> What we think and feel and are, is to a great extent determined by the state of our ductless glands and our viscera.
>
> Aldous Huxley
> "Meditation on El Greco," *Music at Night*, 1931

Brown Rice (or Oat Bran) Cereal

Ingredients:

1. 1 cup brown rice cereal
2. 1 banana
3. A sprinkle of sliced or slivered almonds
4. A sprinkle of unsweetened carob chips
5. 1/2 glass (4 oz.) rice milk or soy milk

Yield: 1 serving

Procedure:

1. Preheat oven to 400 °F .
2. Roast a whole bag of sliced or slivered almonds in a conventional oven for 10 minutes at 400 °F, or in the microwave oven on high heat for 5 minutes. Cool them at room temperature. Then seal them in a plastic bag and put them in the freezer.
3. Pour brown rice cereal in a cereal bowl with a sprinkle of these pre-roasted sliced or slivered almonds.
4. Slice the "just right" banana (not green or too sugary) onto the cereal.
5. Sprinkle unsweetened carob chips and add the rice milk or soy milk in the cereal and enjoy!

Nutritional Benefits:

This is a delicious, quick and nutritious dish for cereal lovers. Brown rice is the least allergic grain among all. For those of you who are allergic to grains, brown rice cereal is a good consideration. Banana is rich in Vitamin A and potassium. Carob chips are rich in vitamins and minerals. For those of you who like chocolate chips, this is a good substitute. Rice milk or soy milk is a good substitute for cow's milk. You may also substitute brown rice cereal with other grains such as oat bran or amaranth flakes. It is a good idea to rotate between different varieties each day.

Brown Rice Gruel

Ingredients:

1. 1 cup short grain brown rice
2. 4 cups purified water
3. A dash of sea salt
4. 1 cup mixed frozen vegetables
   or lima beans

Yield: 4 servings

Procedure:

1. Rinse brown rice twice under running purified water.
2. Put rinsed brown rice, four cups purified water, and a dash of sea salt in a stainless steel or ceramic pot. Cook on low flame (gas stove) or low heat (electric stove).
3. When the rice has boiled and is soft, put in frozen vegetables or lima beans. Let it boil until the mixed vegetables or lima beans are soft and edible.
4. If you have a rice cooker, follow the instructions on p. 34 to cook brown rice. Then, simply put two cups of cooked brown rice together with frozen vegetables and lima beans, and boil until they are soft and edible.

Nutritional Benefits:

Rice gruel is rich in protein, complex carbohydrates, vitamins and fiber. For those of you who are allergic to many grains or have a poor digestive system, rice gruel is good for all three meals. You may alter the variety of vegetables to create a different taste. Serve it with grilled tofu, a pan-fried egg or roasted whole almonds for a main meal, or have one-half cup in between meals as a snack. You may save the leftovers in the refrigerator for no more than three days. If you cannot finish in three days, put the leftovers in small containers (each container good for one meal) and put in the freezer.

Oatmeal or Millet

Ingredients:

1. 1/2 cup oat meal or millet
2. 1 cup purified water
3. 1 banana
4. A sprinkle of pine nuts
5. A sprinkle of carob chips
6. 1 cup rice milk or soy milk (4 oz.)

Yield: 1 Serving

Procedure:

1. Put 1/2 cup of oatmeal or millet in one cup of purified water (a double amount of water) and cook it on the stove in a saucepan, or cook it in the microwave oven in a microwaveable container for two minutes.
2. Pour cooked oatmeal or millet into a serving bowl. Add rice milk or soy milk and stir.
3. Slice "just right" banana into the bowl.
4. Add a sprinkle of pre-roasted pine nuts (use the instructions for roasting sliced or slivered almonds on p. 27).
5. Sprinkle unsweetened carob chips and enjoy!

Nutritional Benefits:

Like brown rice or oat bran cereal, this dish is rich in protein, complex carbohydrates, fiber, vitamins and minerals. Rotate this dish with brown rice or oat bran cereal for variety.

Rye Toast

Ingredients:

1. 1 slice frozen rye bread containing
   no sugar, dairy, wheat nor yeast
2. 1 tablespoon unsweetened apple butter
3. 1 tablespoon unsweetened almond butter
4. 1 glass (8 oz.) rice milk or soy milk, warm
   or cold.

Yield: 1 serving

Procedure:

1. Take one slice of rye bread from the freezer.
2. Put it directly in the toaster on medium heat.
3. When the rye bread is toasted, spread 1 tbs. of unsweetened apple butter and 1 tbs.
   of unsweetened almond butter on it.
4. Enjoy it with a glass of warm or cold rice milk or soy milk.

Nutritional Benefits:

This is a simple breakfast rich in protein, fiber and complex carbohydrates. Instead of spreading a layer of unsweetened apple or almond butter, you also can spread one scrambled egg on it. For those of you who want to watch your weight, one slice of rye toast is sufficient. However, for those of you who want to gain weight or are particularly hungry in the morning, you may use two slices instead of one. You may also use other kinds of bread such as kamut bread, as long as they do not contain sugar, dairy, wheat nor yeast.

Part IV

Lunch and Dinner

Tell me what you eat, and I will tell you who you are.
                              Anthelme Brillat-Savarin
                              Physiologie du gout, 1825

Baked Potatoes or Yam

Ingredients:

1. 4 potatoes or yams
2. Herbal seasoning

Yield: 4 servings

Procedure:

1. Scrub potatoes well with a brush or peel off the skins of yams and rinse.
2. Wrap each potato or yam with tinfoil.
3. Preheat oven to 400 °F.
4. Bake potatoes or yams in a baking pan for one hour at 400 °F.
5. When done, yams can be eaten plain in their entirety. Potatoes can be eaten plain or with a sprinkle of herbal seasoning. You may eat the skins of potatoes if they are organically grown; otherwise, discard them.
6. Serve with other dishes as main meals or eat as a snack.

Nutritional Benefits:

Potatoes or yams are rich in complex carbohydrates, fiber and vitamins. They are the staple food for many ethnic groups. For example, a famous Irish dish is *meat and potatoes*. In the old days (shortly after World War II), farmers in Taiwan relied on yams as a staple food when rice was much more expensive.

Brown Rice

Ingredients:

1. **2 cups short grain brown rice**
2. **4 cups purified water**

Yield: 4 to 6 servings

Procedure:

1. Rinse brown rice twice under running purified water.
2. Put rinsed brown rice in a stainless steel pot or rice cooker and add 4 cups of purified water.
3. If you cook your rice on the stove, use low to medium heat until the rice is done.
4. If you use a rice cooker, the automatic "off switch" will click. Leave the cover on for at least 15 minutes before serving to yield better-tasting rice.
5. Serve the rice with other dishes such as grilled tofu, stir-fried or steamed vegetables and/or soup.
6. If you are watching your weight, have 1/2 cup of brown rice for each meal. Otherwise, you may have a little more. If you save the leftovers in the refrigerator, finish it in three days or less. Otherwise, put it in the freezer.
7. You may use the leftover brown rice to make brown rice gruel (see previous recipe on p.28).

Nutritional Benefits:

Brown rice is rich in complex carbohydrates, fiber, minerals and vitamins especially, vitamin B. In the old days, poor people in Taiwan ate brown rice and more affluent people ate refined, white rice. Ironically, those people who ate brown rice had better health and lower incidents of edema or skin disease. Many researchers also began to use brown rice to facilitate the healing process for people with AIDS. Short grain brown rice has a softer texture; therefore, it tastes better and is easier on the digestion.

Brown Rice Medley

Ingredients:

1. 4 cups cooked brown rice (see previous page for instructions)
2. 2 cups mixed frozen vegetables
3. 1 package baked tofu (11 oz.)
4. 1/2 cup onion, diced
5. 2 tablespoons canola oil
6. A sprinkle of unprocessed sesame oil (dark-colored and with fragrance)
7. 1/4 cup purified water
8. A dash of sea salt
9. 2 tablespoons tamari or Bragg's Liquid Aminos
10. A dash of stevia powder

Yield: 6 to 8 servings

Procedure:

1. Put 2 tbs. of canola oil in a wok or frying pan and use high heat.
2. Wait until oil is hot, then put 1/2 cup of diced onion into it, stir.
3. Pour diced baked tofu into the wok or frying pan and stir with onion.
4. Pour frozen vegetables and 1/4 cup of purified water into the onion and baked tofu mixture. Add a dash of sea salt. Stir and mix all the ingredients well. Cover it and let it simmer for two to three minutes until the frozen vegetables are cooked. Stir a few times to prevent partial burning of the vegetables.
5. Add 2 shakes of stevia, and stir.
6. Add 4 cups of cooked brown rice, and stir.
7. Add 2 tbs. of tamari or Bragg's Liquid Aminos and a sprinkle of sesame oil, and stir.
8. This can be a treat when you have company, or you may save the leftovers in small containers and put them in the freezer. This is also a great lunch item!

Nutritional Benefits:

This dish has fairly complete nutritional value: complex carbohydrates, protein, fiber, vitamins, minerals and unsaturated fat. Some of my previous clients have been eating Brown Rice Medley for lunch, three to five times a week, for five years without getting tired of it!

Curried Potatoes

Ingredients:

1. 2 medium potatoes
2. 2 cups frozen mixed vegetables
3. 1/4 cup onion, shredded
4. 2 tablespoons canola oil
5. 2 cups purified water
6. 2 teaspoons curry powder
7. A dash of sea salt

Yield: 4 servings

Procedure:

1. Peel potatoes. Rinse well, then dice.
2. Put 2 tbs. of canola oil in a wok or frying pan. Use high heat.
3. Wait until oil is hot, then add shredded onion and stir.
4. Pour frozen mixed vegetables and 2 cups of purified water into the wok or frying pan and stir. Add a dash of sea salt and curry powder and stir again.
5. Cover it and let it simmer for about five minutes. Mix all the ingredients well, stir a few times until the potatoes and mixed vegetables are cooked.
6. Serve with brown rice.

Nutritional Benefits:

This dish is designed for people who like spicy-hot food. You may adjust the amount of curry to suit your tastes. This dish is rich in complex carbohydrates, vitamins and minerals. It tastes great served with brown rice!

Egg Foo Yong

Ingredients:

1. 3 eggs
2. 1/2 cup onion, diced
3. 2 cups green bean sprouts
4. 1 carrot

5. 4 tablespoons canola oil
6. A dash of sea salt
7. A dash of stevia
8. A sprinkle of purified water

Yield: 4 servings

Procedure:

1. Rinse green bean sprouts well. You may leave the root on, or pinch it off.
2. Dice the onion.
3. Peel carrot. Rinse it, and then grate it.
4. Beat all three eggs with a fork, chopsticks or eggbeater.
5. Put 1 tbs. of canola oil in a wok or frying pan and sauté the diced onion. When you can smell the fragrance of the onion, put bean sprouts, grated carrot and a dash of sea salt into the onion and stir. Sprinkle purified water and stir some more.
6. Take the whole mixture out of the wok or frying pan and pour it into the beaten eggs. Add a dash of sea salt and two shakes of stevia and mix all the ingredients well.
7. Put 2 tbs. of canola oil in a non-stick frying pan. Wait until oil is hot, then pour the whole mixture into the frying pan.
8. Wait until the bottom side is golden-brown, then flip it over to a large, round dish. Put one tbs. of canola oil in the frying pan, and slip the uncooked side of the egg foo yong back into the frying pan. When the bottom is golden-brown, it is done.
9. Cut into 8 slices and serve with brown rice and other vegetables.

Nutritional Benefits:

This dish is rich in protein, fiber, vitamins and unsaturated fat. For those of you who get hungry easily, this dish will give you longer-lasting satisfaction.

Ginger-Onion-Garlic Chicken

Ingredients:

1. 8 oz. skinless chicken
2. 1 tablespoon canola oil
3. A sprinkle of unprocessed sesame oil
4. 1 slice ginger
5. 2 slices onion
6. 1 clove garlic
7. 2 tablespoons tamari or Bragg's Liquid Aminos
8. 1/8 cup purified water

Yield: 2 servings

Procedure:

1. Remove the skin and fat from the chicken. Rinse well, then cut into small pieces.
2. Rinse ginger, and then cut into fine pieces.
3. Dice onion.
4. Mince garlic.
5. Put 1 tbs. of canola oil in a wok or frying pan. Use high heat. Wait until oil is hot, then put in ginger, onion and garlic.
5. When you can smell their fragrance, add chicken and stir.
6. Pour in purified water and tamari (or Bragg's Liquid Aminos) and stir. Cover it and let it simmer for three minutes.
7. Uncover, stir again. Sprinkle in some unprocessed sesame oil and stir some more. If the chicken is not done, cover it and cook one or two more minutes. When the chicken is cooked, serve with brown rice and other vegetable dishes.

Nutritional Benefits:

This dish is rich in protein. It also contains saturated fat. Only prepare this dish when you are weaning yourself off of meat. Have this dish only once or twice a week.

Ginger-Onion Fish

Ingredients:

1. 8 oz. salmon, halibut or cod steak
2. 1 slice of ginger, julienne
3. 2 slices of onion, julienne
4. 2 tablespoons canola oil
5. 2 tablespoons tamari or Bragg's Liquid Aminos
6. 1/8 cup purified water
7. A dash of sea salt

Yield: 2 servings

Procedure:

1. Remove the skin from the fish, and rinse the fish well. Smear some sea salt sparingly on both sides of the fish steak.
2. Put 1 tbs. of canola oil in a non-stick frying pan. Use high heat.
3. Wait until oil is hot, then add ginger and onion and stir.
4. When you smell their fragrance, take out ginger and onion and put the fish in the frying pan.
5. Put the ginger and onion back on top of the fish. Reduce the heat to medium. Cover the fish and cook until the bottom is golden-brown.
6. Flip over the fish and put ginger and onion on top of the fish steak. Put 1 tbs. of canola oil in the frying pan after the fish steak has been flipped over.
7. When the bottom is golden-brown, put in 2 tbs. of tamari or Bragg's Liquid Aminos and 1/8 cup of purified water. Cover it and let it simmer for one minute or so with ginger and onion in the sauce.
8. Serve with brown rice and vegetable dishes.

Nutritional Benefits:

This dish is rich in protein and fish oil. Use only cold-water fish to reduce the possibility of bacterial, yeast and parasitic infections. Avoid having this dish more than twice a week.

Grilled Tofu

Ingredients:

1. A container hard tofu
2. 2 tablespoons canola oil
3. 2 tablespoons tamari or Bragg's Liquid Aminos
4. 2 stalks green onion (scallions)
5. A dash of stevia powder
6. 1/4 cup purified water

Yield: 4 servings

Procedure:

1. Empty out the water in the tofu container. Rinse tofu with purified water.
2. Slice tofu into about 2-inch long, 1-1/2-inch wide, and 1/2-inch thick pieces.
3. Pour 2 tbs. of canola oil in a flat, non-stick frying pan. Use medium heat. Wait until oil is hot, then gently lay each piece of tofu in the pan and line them up. Avoid overlapping.
4. When the bottoms are golden-brown, flip each piece over gently with a spatula.
5. Rinse green onion well. Discard the head (roots) and outer layers. Use only the clean, healthy-looking part. Cut into two-inch segments.
6. When both sides of tofu are golden-brown, add 2 tbs. of tamari or Bragg's Liquid Aminos, 1/4 cup of purified water and a few segments of cleaned green onion. Stir gently and then cover the frying pan and allow to simmer for one minute.
7. Remove the lid, and add two shakes of stevia. Stir gently, and then put it in a dish. Serve with brown rice and vegetable dishes.

Nutritional Benefits:

Tofu is rich in lecithin, protein minerals and vitamins. These nutrients are essential in building muscles and nourishing the brain. Many researchers are using lecithin to help AIDS clients build their immunity. Stevia is a natural sweetener which is excellent in regenerating the pancreas and thus is particularly helpful to people with diabetes or hypoglycemia.

Oriental Salad

Ingredients:

1. 1 cup carrots, julienne
2. 1 cup cucumber, julienne
3. 2 cups green bean sprouts
4. 1 baked tofu (brown color)
5. 3 teaspoons tamari
6. 1 teaspoon unprocessed sesame oil

Yield: 4 servings

Procedure:

1. Peel carrots, rinse well and then julienne.
2. Scrub cucumbers well with a brush. Cut off the tips of both ends. Cut cucumbers in half (longitudinally) and remove seeds, and then julienne.
3. Rinse green bean sprouts well, put in boiling water and stir for a few seconds and then drain water.
4. Put the whole piece of baked tofu in the saucepan. Add 2 tsp. of tamari and enough purified water to cover baked tofu. Boil on low heat for a minute or two. Cut baked tofu into thin strips.
5. Mix ingredients together with 1 tsp. of tamari and unprocessed sesame oil.

Nutritional Benefits:

This is a good dish for raw vegetable lovers. It's easy to make and rich in fiber, vitamins A and C, protein and beta carotene. It's great for a hot summer day!

Rice Noodle Delight

Ingredients:

1. 16 oz. dry rice noodles
2. 4 oz. dry tofu skin
3. 1/2 cup onion, julienne
4. 1 cup carrots, julienne
5. 1 cup shredded cabbage
6. 1 cup thin celery strips
7. 4 tablespoons canola oil
8. 2 teaspoons unprocessed sesame oil
9. 1 tablespoon tamari
10. A dash of sea salt

Yield: 4 servings

Procedure:

1. Soak dry rice noodles in hot water.
2. Soak tofu skin in hot water. When it is soft, cut into 1-1/2-inch-long strips.
3. Put 2 tbs. of canola oil in the wok or frying pan. When oil is hot, put in onion and stir. When you can smell the flavor of the onion, add the rest of the vegetables and tofu skins and stir. Add a pinch of sea salt and sprinkle with purified water, then cover it and simmer for a minute. Uncover, stir again and put the vegetables in a big dish.
4. Clean the wok or frying pan, dry it with a paper towel and then put 2 tbs. of canola oil in it. Drain the soaked rice noodles and put them in the wok. Stir, put in 1 tbs. of tamari, and stir again. Then mix the cooked vegetables with the rice noodles, add 2 tsp. of unprocessed sesame oil.
5. When the noodles are soft and edible, transfer to serving dishes.

Nutritional Benefits:

This dish is a complete meal! It contains complex carbohydrates, fiber, vitamins, minerals, protein and unsaturated fat. Serve with a cup of soup or a cup of caffeine-free herbal tea. For people who love spaghetti, macaroni or wheat noodles, this is a great substitute!

Steamed Fish

Ingredients:

1. 8 oz. cod or halibut fillet
2. 1 slice ginger
3. 2 slices onion
4. A dash of sea salt
5. 1 tablespoon tamari

Yield: 2 servings

Procedure:

1. Rinse fish well. Dry it with a paper towel. Smear sea salt sparingly on both sides of the fish steak. Put it in a ceramic dish.
2. Rinse ginger and onion well and cut into thin strips. Put the ginger and onion strips on top of the fish.
3. Sprinkle 1 tbs. of tamari on the fish.
4. Put the dish in a steamer and steam for 45 minutes.

Nutritional Benefits:

This dish is rich in protein, fish oil and minerals. You may alternate between different kinds of cold-water fish. Serve with brown rice, vegetables and soup.

Steamed Vegetables

Ingredients:

1. 2 carrots, sliced
2. 1 cup broccoli, large flowerets
3. 1 cup cauliflower, large flowerets
4. 1 cup zucchini, sliced
5. 1 teaspoon tamari
6. A sprinkle of unprocessed sesame oil

Yield: 4 servings

Procedure:

1. Peel carrots. Rinse well, and slice.
2. Rinse broccoli and cauliflower well under running purified water, and cut into large flowerets.
3. Wash zucchini well with a brush, and slice.
4. Put all the vegetables in a ceramic dish and steam in a steamer, or in a wok with a steam tray in between the dish and the water. Steam for five minutes after the water has boiled.
5. When the vegetables are lightly cooked, sprinkle tamari and a few drops of unprocessed sesame oil. Mix well and serve with brown rice, grilled tofu and soup.

Nutritional Benefits:

This dish is rich in fiber, vitamins and minerals. Eat the vegetables when they are hot to enjoy the flavor. Consume the whole dish in one meal. The taste and nutritional values of leftover steamed vegetables are not very good. Alternate with a variety of vegetables.

Stir-Fried Vegetables

Ingredients:

1. 2 carrots, sliced
2. 1 cup broccoli, large flowerets
3. 1 cup cauliflower, large flowerets
4. 1 cup zucchini, sliced
5. 1/4 cup onion, shredded
6. 2 tablespoons canola oil
7. A dash of sea salt
8. A dash of stevia powder
9. Unprocessed sesame oil

Yield: 4 servings

Procedure:

1. Peel carrots. Rinse well, and slice.
2. Rinse broccoli and cauliflower well under running purified water, and cut into large flowerets.
3. Wash zucchini well with a brush, and slice.
4. Pour 2 tbs. of canola oil in a wok or frying pan. Wait until oil is hot, then put in onion and stir.
5. When you smell the fragrance of the onion, put in carrots and stir. Then, put in broccoli, cauliflower, a dash of sea salt and a sprinkle of purified water, and stir.
6. Put in zucchini and stir. Cover the vegetables for one minute.
7. Remove the lid; add two shakes of stevia and stir.
8. Add a few drops of sesame oil and stir some more. Serve with brown rice, grilled tofu and soup.

Nutritional Benefits:

This dish is rich in fiber, vitamins and minerals. Once you get used to eating lightly cooked vegetables, you may not miss salad (raw vegetables) any more. The oil you use in stir-fry will seal the nutrients and the flavor of the vegetables. Therefore, if you save a portion from dinner for lunch the following day, the nutrients and flavor of this dish will remain intact even after heating in the microwave oven. Alternate with a variety of vegetables.

Tofu Supreme

Ingredients:

1. 2 carrots, grated
2. 1 medium green pepper, diced
3. 1/4 cup onion, diced
4. 1 tub hard tofu
5. 1 tablespoon canola oil
6. A dash of sea salt
7. A sprinkle of unprocessed sesame oil
8. A sprinkle of tamari
9. A sprinkle of purified water

Yield: 4 servings

Procedure:

1. Peel carrots. Rinse well, and grate.
2. Wash green pepper well with a brush. Remove seeds and dice.
3. Pour 1 tbs. of canola oil in a wok or frying pan. Wait until oil is hot, then put in diced onion and stir.
4. When you smell the fragrance of the onion, put in carrots, green pepper, a dash of sea salt and a sprinkle of purified water, and stir.
5. Remove water from tub and rinse tofu with purified water. Smash tofu and mix it well with the vegetables in the wok or frying pan.
6. Add a sprinkle of sesame oil and tamari, and stir. Serve with brown rice and soup.

Nutritional Benefits:

This dish is rich in protein, fiber, vitamins and minerals. You may serve it with brown rice or use it as a spread for sandwich.

Part V

Sandwiches

Man is the only animal that can remain on friendly terms with the victims he intends to eat until he eats them.

Samuel Butler
"Mind and Matter," *Note-Books*, 1912

Avocado Sandwich

Ingredients:

1. 1 soft avocado
2. 1 carrot, grated
3. 1 celery stalk, sliced
4. 1/2 cup unsalted sunflower seeds, pre-roasted
5. 1/2 cup chopped walnuts, pre-roasted
6. 8 slices of rye or kamut bread (containing no sugar, dairy, wheat nor yeast)

Yield: 4 servings

Procedure:

1. Remove the seed and skin of the avocado. Smash it in a mixing bowl.
2. Peel carrot, rinse and grate.
3. Wash celery well with a brush. Cut into thin slices.
4. Roast sunflower seeds and walnuts in a microwave oven or conventional oven. (See instructions in previous recipe on p. 27.)
5. Mix carrot, celery, sunflower seeds and walnuts with avocado.
6. Toast bread on medium heat.
7. Spread the avocado mix on the bread. Serve with a cup of herbal tea, or a glass of rice milk or soy milk.

Nutritional Benefits:

This sandwich is rich in protein, fiber, vitamins, complex carbohydrates and unsaturated fat. Great for sandwich lovers. You may enjoy this sandwich as a lunch or a snack.

Lentil Sandwich

Ingredients:

1. 1 cup lentils
2. 1 cup carrot, grated
3. 1/2 cup onion, diced
4. 1 cup green pepper, diced
5. 1 tablespoon canola oil
6. A dash of sea salt
7. A dash of stevia powder.
8. Purified water
9. 8 slices of rye or kamut bread (containing no sugar, dairy, wheat nor yeast)

Yield: 4 servings

Procedure:

1. Rinse lentils well with purified water. Then soak lentils in 2 cups of purified water in a stainless steel pot for about one hour.
2. Add a dash of sea salt and cook lentils with soaking water on low heat.
3. Pour 1 tbs. of canola oil in the wok or frying pan. Wait until oil is hot, then put in diced onion and stir.
4. When you smell the fragrance of the onion, put in carrot, green pepper, a dash of sea salt and a sprinkle of purified water, and stir.
5. When lentils are cooked, drain excess water and smash them into a paste.
6. Mix the vegetables with the lentil paste and with two shakes of stevia powder.
7. Toast 8 pieces of rye or kamut bread on medium heat.
8. Spread the lentil paste on the bread.

Nutritional Benefits:

This sandwich is rich in protein, fiber, vitamins, minerals and complex carbohydrates. Great for lunch or snack.

Salmon Sandwich

Ingredients:

1. 4 oz. salmon
2. 1/2 celery stalk, diced
3. 1/4 cup chopped walnuts, pre-roasted
4. A pinch of sea salt
5. A dash of stevia powder
6. 4 slices rye or kamut bread
   (containing no sugar, dairy, wheat
   nor yeast)

Yield: 2 servings

Procedure:

1. Remove skin and rinse salmon well. Boil in purified water for three minutes or until cooked.
2. Wash and prepare celery.
3. Smash cooked salmon in a mixing bowl. Add diced celery, pre-roasted chopped walnuts (see instructions for roasting nuts on p. 27), sea salt and 2 shakes of stevia, and mix well.
4. Toast rye or kamut bread on medium heat.
5. Spread the salmon mixture on the bread. Serve with a cup of hot caffeine-free herbal tea or soup.

Nutritional Benefits:

This sandwich is rich in protein, fish oil, fiber and minerals. A great substitute for tuna-fish sandwich. This dish is easy to prepare and delicious and nutritious as a lunch or a snack.

Tofu Supreme Sandwich

Ingredients:

1. 2 carrots, grated
2. 1 medium green pepper, diced
3. 1/4 cup onion, diced
4. 1 tub hard tofu
5. 1 tablespoon canola oil
6. A sprinkle of tamari
7. A dash of sea salt
8. A sprinkle of unprocessed sesame oil
9. 1 teaspoon tapioca powder
10. A sprinkle of purified water
11. 8 slices rye or kamut bread (containing no sugar, dairy, wheat nor yeast)

Yield: 4 servings

Procedure:

1. Follow the procedure from 1 through 6 on p. 46.
2. Mix tapioca powder with 2 tsp. of purified water, then pour it into the tofu mixture.
3. Stir well until the mixture sticks together.
4. Toast bread on medium heat.
5. Spread the tofu mixture on the bread.

Nutritional Benefits:

This sandwich is rich in protein, fiber, vitamins, minerals and complex carbohydrates. Another filling dish for sandwich lovers.

Part VI

Soups

Americans can eat garbage, provided you sprinkle it liberally with ketchup, mustard, chili sauce, Tabasco sauce, cayenne pepper, or any other condiment which destroys the original flavor of the dish.

Henry Miller
"The Staff of Life," *Remember to Remember*, 1947

Barley Soup

Ingredients:

1. 1 cup dry barley
2. 1 cup carrots, diced
3. 1/2 cup celery, diced
4. 1/2 cup broccoli, small flowerets
5. 1/2 cup cauliflower, small flowerets
6. 1/2 cup onion, diced
7. A dash of sea salt
8. 3 cups purified water

Yield: 4 servings

Procedure:

1. Rinse barley well and soak in 3 cups of purified water in a stainless steel pot for about an hour.
2. Wash and prepare the vegetables.
3. Add a dash of sea salt to barley and cook it on the stove on low heat.
4. When barley is boiled, add the vegetables and stir. Cover the pot and cook on high heat for one minute.
5. Uncover, and stir a few times. Serve with brown rice and other dishes.

Nutritional Benefits:

This dish is rich in complex carbohydrates, fiber, vitamins and minerals. Very satisfying and easy on the digestion. Great for lunch, dinner or snack.

Cauliflower Soup

Ingredients:

1. 2 cups cauliflower, large flowerets
2. 1/2 cup carrots, sliced
3. 1 cup fried tofu (puffed)
4. A dash of sea salt
5. 3 cups purified water
6. A dash of stevia powder
7. A sprinkle of unprocessed sesame oil

Yield: 4 servings

Procedure:

1. Wash and prepare cauliflower in large flowerets.
2. Put peeled and sliced carrots together with cauliflower, fried tofu and a dash of sea salt in 3 cups of purified water and cook on high heat with the cover on.
3. When the content has boiled, uncover. Add 2 shakes of stevia and a sprinkle of unprocessed sesame oil, and stir.

Nutritional Benefits:

This dish is rich in vitamins A and C and dietary indoles. Cauliflower is part of the crucifer family which is an excellent antioxidant. Fried tofu is rich in lecithin and gives a long-lasting satisfaction. This dish is very low in calories and easy to make. For those who like to have low-calorie, clear soup, this dish is an excellent choice.

Green Bean (Mung Bean) Noodle Soup

Ingredients:

1. 1 small pack of dry green (mung) bean noodles (about 1.4 oz)
2. 1/2 cup carrots, julienne
3. 1/2 cup celery, julienne
4. 1 egg (optional)
5. 1 stalk green onion (scallion), sliced
6. A sprinkle of unprocessed sesame oil
7. A dash of sea salt.
8. A dash of stevia powder
9. 4 cups purified water

Yield: 4 servings

Procedure:

1. Boil 4 cups of purified water in a pot on high heat.
2. Wash and prepare the vegetables.
3. Use a pair of scissors to cut the dry green (mung) bean noodles into approximately 4-inch long segments. When the water has boiled, put these dry noodles into the water with a dash of sea salt.
4. When the green (mung) bean soup has boiled, put in carrots, celery and 2 shakes of stevia, and stir.
5. Beat the egg and pour it into the soup. Wait until the egg firms up, then stir and mix well with the rest of the ingredients.
6. Add sliced scallions and a sprinkle of unprocessed sesame oil and serve with brown rice and other dishes.

Nutritional Benefits:

This dish is low in calories, and rich in complex carbohydrates, fiber, vitamins and protein. A great dish as a snack or main meal.

Lentil Soup

Ingredients:

1. 1 cup dry lentils
2. 1 cup carrots, diced
3. 1/2 cup celery, diced
4. 1/2 cup broccoli, small flowerets
5. 1/2 cup cauliflower, small flowerets
6. 1/2 cup onion, diced
7. A dash of sea salt
8. 3 cups purified water

Yield: 4 servings

Procedure:

1. Wash lentils well and rinse off the water several times until it is clear. Soak lentils in 3 cups of purified water in a stainless steel pot for about an hour.
2. Put a dash of sea salt in lentils and cook on low heat with the lid on.
3. wash and prepare the vegetables.
4. When lentils are boiled, put in all the vegetables and mix well. Put the lid back on the pot and cook on high heat for one minute or two. Serve with brown rice, a sanwich or other dishes.

Nutritional Benefits:

This dish is complete with protein, complex carbohydrates, vitamins, minerals and fiber. Very satisfying for lunch, dinner or snack. Sometimes when you don't feel like having a full meal, add 1/2 cup of cooked brown rice to the soup and boil for a minute. This is a great choice for a light meal.

Rice Noodle Soup

Ingredients:

1. 8 oz. dry rice noodle
2. 1 cup carrots, julienne
3. 1 cup cabbage, shredded
4. 1 cup celery, julienne
5. 1 cup green bean sprouts
6. 1/2 cup fried tofu
7. 1/4 cup Chinese pickled mustard greens
8. A dash of sea salt
9. A sprinkle of dark sesame oil
10. A sprinkle of dry Chinese onion
11. 2 eggs (optional)
12. 4 cups purified water

Yield: 4 servings

Procedure:

1. Soak rice noodle in boiled water.
2. Wash and prepare the vegetables. Cut fried tofu into wide strips. Cut Chinese pickled mustard greens into thin strips.
3. Put cabbage and a dash of sea salt in 4 cups of purified water in a pot and cook on high heat with the lid on.
4. When the content has boiled, put in rice noodle, carrots and celery, and bring it to boil.
5. Put in green bean sprouts, fried tofu and Chinese pickled mustard greens. Stir and mix well.
6. Pour in beaten eggs. Wait until the eggs begin to firm up, then stir and mix it well with the soup content.
7. Sprinkle some dry Chinese onion and dark (unprocessed) sesame oil into the soup.

Nutritional Benefits:

This dish is complete with complex carbohydrates, protein, vitamins, minerals and fiber. This a wonderful substitute for wheat noodle soup. For those who love spaghetti or Chinese wheat noodles, this is a great alternative! This can be served as a complete meal or a snack.

Split Pea Soup

Ingredients:

1. 1 cup dry split peas
2. 1 cup carrots, diced
3. 1/2 cup celery, diced
4. 1/2 cup broccoli, small flowerets
5. 1/2 cup cauliflower, small flowerets
6. 1/2 cup onion, diced
7. A dash of sea salt
8. 3 cups purified water

Yield: 4 servings

Procedure:

1. Wash split peas well and rinse off the water several times until it is clear. Soak split peas in 3 cups of purified water in a stainless steel pot for about an hour.
2. Put a dash of sea salt in split peas and cook on low heat with the lid on.
3. wash and prepare the vegetables.
4. When split peas are boiled, put in all the vegetables and mix well. Put the lid back on the pot and cook on high heat for one minute or two. Serve with brown rice, a sandwich or other dishes.

Nutritional Benefits:

Like lentil soup, this dish is complete with protein, complex carbohydrates, vitamins, minerals and fiber. Very satisfying for lunch, dinner or snack. Sometimes when you don't feel like having a full meal, add 1/2 cup of cooked brown rice to the soup and boil for a minute. This is a great choice for a light meal.

Tofu-Seaweed Soup

Ingredients:

1. 1/2 tub hard tofu
2. 2 sheets dry seaweed (flaky type)
3. 1/2 cup carrots, sliced
4. 1 slice ginger
5. A dash of sea salt
6. A dash of stevia powder
7. A sprinkle of unprocessed sesame oil
8. 3 cups purified water

Yield: 4 servings

Procedure:

1. Cut ginger into thin strips. Put it in 3 cups of purified water together with peeled and sliced carrots and a dash of sea salt in a stainless steel or ceramic pot. Boil the content on high heat.
2. Rinse off water from the tub and cut tofu into about one-inch long, 1/2-inch wide and 1/2-inch thick dice. (Put some purified water in the tub and save the leftover tofu in the refrigerator. Use the leftover tofu within three days.)
3. Bring the content to boil, and put in tofu. Cut seaweed into pieces (or tear with your fingers) and drop them into the soup.
4. Add 2 shakes of stevia and a sprinkle of unprocessed sesame oil, and stir. Serve with brown rice and other dishes.

Nutritional Benefits:

Some people love this dish, others hate it! This dish is very rich in protein and minerals, especially iodine. Iodine is excellent for metabolic function of the thyroid. It is also helpful for growing healthy hair, skin and nails. For those of you who don't mind the fishy taste of seaweed, this dish is great for weight watchers because it is low in calories, rich in protein and great for metabolic function!

Vegetable Soup

Ingredients:

1. 1/2 cup onion, diced
2. 1 cup frozen mixed vegetables
3. 1 medium potato
4. 1/2 cup cauliflower, small flowerets
5. 1/2 cup broccoli, small flowerets
6. 1/2 cup celery, diced
7. A dash of sea salt
8. 5 cups purified water

Yield: 4 servings

Procedure:

1. Peel the potato. Rinse well, then dice.
2. Put frozen mixed vegetables, potatoes and a dash of a sea salt in 5 cups of purified water and boil in a pot on high heat with the lid on.
3. Wash and prepare cauliflower, broccoli, celery and onion.
4. After the content has boiled, taste the potatoes. When they are soft and edible, put in cauliflower, broccoli, celery and onion. Mix well. Let it boil with the lid on for another minute. Serve with brown rice, a sandwich or other dishes.

Nutritional Benefits:

This dish is rich in complex carbohydrates, protein, vitamins, minerals and fiber. It is very filling and satisfying. This is an all-time favorite for all ages and ethnic groups.

White Radish Soup

Ingredients:

1. 1 medium white radish
2. 1 cup carrots, sliced
3. 1 cup fried tofu (puffed)
4. A few stalks of cilantro
5. A dash of sea salt
6. A dash of stevia powder
7. 4 cups purified water

Yield: 4 servings

Procedure:

1. Peel the skin off the white radish. Wash well, then cut into approximately 2-inch long, 1-inch wide and 1/2-inch thick pieces.
2. Put white radish, fried tofu and a dash of sea salt in 4 cups of purified water in a stainless steel or ceramic pot. Boil the content on high heat for two minutes with the lid on.
3. When the soup has boiled, add carrots and boil for another minute.
4. Wash cilantro well and cut into small segments.
5. Lift the cover and taste white radish. When it is soft, it is done. Add 2 shakes of stevia and cilantro into the soup. Stir, and serve with brown rice and other dishes.

Nutritional Benefits:

This dish is rich in vitamins, protein and fiber. According to Chinese medicine, this dish is good for cleansing and reducing anxiety and fever.

> With health, you can do anything; without health, nothing else matters.

Part VII

Desserts

One cannot think well, love well, sleep well, if one has not dined well.

Virginia Woolf
A Room of One's Own, 1929

Oat Bran Cookies

Ingredients:

1. 1 cup oat bran
2. 1/2 cup rice bran
3. 1/2 cup purified water
4. 1/4 cup brown rice syrup
5. 1/4 cup chopped pecans, pre-roasted
6. 1/4 cup canola oil
7. 1 tablespoon baking powder
8. 1 teaspoon vanilla extract
9. 1/8 teaspoon stevia powder
10. 1/2 cup unsweetened carob chips

Yield: 10 -12 cookies

Procedure:

1. Preheat oven to 350 °F.
2. Mix all the ingredients in a large mixing bowl (see instructions for roasting nuts on p. 27).
3. Spoon dough onto an oiled cookie sheet. Use a cookie cutter and a wet spoon to shape the cookies nicely.
4. Decorate top of cookies with unsweetened carob chips.
5. Bake at 350 °F for 25 minutes or until golden brown.

Nutritional Benefits:

This cookie contains no sugar, dairy, wheat, yeast, egg nor salt. It is rich in fiber and complex carbohydrates. It is a nice treat to have one oat bran cookie with a cup of hot caffeine-free herbal tea as a morning or afternoon snack. It is also safe for diabetics to enjoy!

Brownies

Ingredients:

1. 1 cup brown rice flower
2. 1 cup brown rice bran
3. 1 cup chopped walnuts, pre-roasted
4. 1 cup purified water
5. 1/2 cup brown rice syrup
6. 1/4 cup roasted carob powder
7. 1 tablespoon baking powder
8. 1/4 cup canola oil
9. 1 teaspoon vanilla extract
10. 1/8 teaspoon stevia powder

Yield: 9 brownies

Procedure:

1. Preheat oven to 350 °F.
2. Mix all ingredients well in a large mixing bowl (see instructions for roasting nuts on p. 27) until achieving a thick consistency.
3. Pour the mixture into an oiled 8-inch square baking pan.
4. Bake at 350 °F for 60 minutes or until a toothpick comes out clean.
5. Set on the rack to cool.
6. Use a sharp knife to cut into 9 square pieces.

Nutritional Benefits:

This dessert is rich in complex carbohydrates, minerals, protein and flavor. For those of you who are chocolate lovers, this is a great substitute! It is a delicious morning or afternoon snack with a cup of hot caffeine-free herbal tea!

Oat Bran Muffins

Ingredients:

1. 1-1/2 cups rice bran
2. 1 cup oat bran
3. 1/2 cup brown rice flour
4. 1 tablespoon baking powder
5. 1/4 cup canola oil
6. 1-3/4 cup purified water
7. 1/2 cup brown rice syrup
8. 1 teaspoon vanilla extract
9. 1/4 teaspoon stevia powder
10. 1/2 cup chopped walnuts, pre-roasted
11. 1/8 cup unsweetened carob chips

Yield: 6 muffins

Procedure:

1. Preheat oven to 350 °F.
2. Mix all ingredients (see instructions for roasting nuts on p. 27) in a large mixing bowl.
3. Pour mixture in an oiled muffin pan.
4. Bake at 350 °F for 40 minutes or until a toothpick comes out clean.
5. Set on the rack to cool.

Nutritional Benefits:

This delicious muffin is rich in complex carbohydrates, fiber, minerals and protein. You may enjoy it as a breakfast or a snack.

Banana Ice Cream

Ingredients:

1. 4 ripe bananas
2. 4 whole walnuts, pre-roasted

Yield: 4 servings

Procedure:

1. Peel ripe bananas. Seal them in a plastic bag and put in the freezer overnight.
2. Put one banana in a Champion juicer and turn on the switch.
3. As the banana ice cream comes out from the other end of the juicer, use a serving cup to catch it. Rotate the cup slowly to create a nice twirl. Repeat the same procedure for each banana.
4. Put a roasted whole walnut (see instructions for roasting nuts on p. 27) on top of banana ice cream and serve immediately.

Nutritional Benefits:

Banana is rich in vitamin A which is great for the eyesight. Banana can also help you eliminate smoothly. This dessert is great during the hot summer season, especially when you have company.

Green Bean Soup

Ingredients:

1. 1 cup dry green beans
2. 4 cup purified water
3. 1/2 cup dry lotus seeds
4. 1 cup brown rice syrup

Yield: 4 servings

Procedure:

1. Rinse dry green beans and lotus seeds well under running purified water several times.
2. Pour 4 cups of purified water on green beans and lotus seeds in a pot and boil on low heat with the lid on.
3. When the green beans pop open and the lotus seeds are soft and edible, add brown rice syrup and stir well.
4. You may serve this dessert hot, cold or at room temperature.

Nutritional Benefits:

This dish is rich in protein, complex carbohydrates, fiber and vitamins. This dish will please your sweet tooth and also cleanse your system especially during the summertime.

Red Bean Soup

Ingredients:

1. 1 cup dry Chinese red beans
2. 4 cup purified water
3. 1/2 cup dry Chinese red or black dates
4. 1 cup brown rice syrup

Yield: 4 servings

Procedure:

1. Rinse dry Chinese red beans and red or black dates well under running purified water several times.
2. Pour 4 cups of purified water on red beans in a pot and boil on low heat with the lid on.
3. When the red beans pop open, put in the dates and let the soup boil for another minute or two.
4. When the dates are puffed and soft, add brown rice syrup and stir well.
5. You may serve this dessert hot or at room temperature.

Nutritional Benefits:

This dish is rich in protein, complex carbohydrates, fiber and vitamins. This dish will please your sweet tooth and also warm up your system especially during the wintertime.

Part VIII

Beverages

> Hunger does not breed reform; it breeds madness and all the ugly distempers that make an ordered life impossible.
>
> Woodrow Wilson
> *Address to Congress*, 1918

As explained in my book, ***Breaking the Yeast Curse: Food and Unconditional Love for Magic Healing,*** it is essential to have 8 to 10 cups (8 oz. each) of fluid per day to ensure the smooth function of your "sewage system "-- your digestive and urinary tracts. The beverages recommended in Dr. J's anti-yeast nutritional program include:

* **Purified Water**
* **Caffeine-Free Herbal Tea**
* **Rice Milk**
* **Soy Milk**
* **Unsweetened Apple Juice**
* **Vegetable Juices**
* **Other Beverages**

It is recommended that you drink these beverages warm or at room temperature. When the temperature of the beverage is too cold or too hot, it can "shock" your digestive system and cause discomfort.

Purified Water:

Bottled water or water from a purifier installed in your kitchen is a good choice. Distilled water is not recommended because it does not contain minerals. If you use a water purifier, choose the type with reverse osmosis. A water purifier with reverse osmosis usually does a better job to filter out the odor, bacteria, yeasts, parasites and chemicals.

Caffeine-Free Herbal Teas:

Nowadays, all supermarkets, health food stores and most restaurants carry caffeine-free herbal teas. If you don't like the plain taste of water, try out different kinds of caffeine-free herbal teas. You may carry your herbal tea to work by steeping a tea bag in a thermos with boiled water. You may also steep a tea bag in a pot of boiled water and let it sit on the warmer if you have a coffee maker at home or in your office. This will give you a sufficient supply of warm herbal tea all day long.

Rice Milk:

Rice milk is the juice produced from grinding rice and filtering out the pulp. For people whose bodies are highly allergic or sensitive, rice milk is a good choice of beverage, for rice is the least allergy-causing item among all foods. Rice milk is available in most health food stores. If you cannot find it, request that your local health food stores or supermarkets carry them. When the stores get enough requests, they will begin to carry the item as it is in great demand.

Soy Milk:

Soy milk is the juice produced from grinding soy (yellow) beans and filtering out the pulp. Soy milk is rich in protein and lecithin, an essential element for the growth and repair of body cells. Nowadays, many babies are fed with soy formulas instead of cow milk formulas. Most health food stores and supermarkets carry soy milk with plain, vanilla and chocolate flavors.

Unsweetened Apple Juice:

Although fruit juices are rich in vitamin C, most of them contain a high concentration of fructose which turns into sugar in your body. They also contain yeasts because of the way they are juiced. If you must have fruit juice, make your own apple juice (after washing the apples well).

Vegetable Juices:

If you enjoy vegetable juicing, 4 ounces of carrot juice mixed with 4 ounces of celery juice is a good combination. Straight carrot juice contains a large amount of natural sugar, and straight celery juice contains a large amount of natural sodium. The carrot and celery juice mixture makes a good blend and balance. Have this juice mixture only once or twice a week.

Other Beverages:

The green bean or red bean soup described in the **Desserts** section can also be used as beverages. You can also put a banana or a slice of ripe papaya and a glass (6 to 8 oz.) of soy milk or rice milk in a blender to make a nice shake. Be creative!

"Diseases enter through your mouth; while disasters outpour from your mouth." It pays to watch carefully what goes in and what comes out!

Part IX

Frequently Asked Questions (FAQs) about Dr. J's Anti-Yeast Nutritional Program

I have no doubt that it is a part of the destiny of the human race, in its gradual improvement, to leave off eating animals, as surely as the savage tribes have left off eating each other when they came in contact with the more civilized.

Thoreau
"Higher Laws," *Walden,* 1854

Q: How long should I stay on Dr. J's anti-yeast nutritional program?

A: It depends on how long you want to live! The anti-yeast nutritional program is not a "temporary diet." Instead, it is a nutritional program for life! As long as you want to be free of yeast symptoms, you need to stay on this anti-yeast nutritional program.

Q: Can I eat "regular" food once my yeast disorder symptoms are under control?

A: In order for your body to cleanse toxins and regenerate the functions of your organs and glands, you should *stay on Dr. J's anti-yeast nutritional program strictly for at least three to six months.* When you are relatively symptom-free, then you can "relax" a little bit. Once in a while, you may taste "regular" food, but do not indulge. If you cannot exercise your willpower, then don't take the chance! Going back to your "regular" food is just like going back to drinking or smoking; it is not easy to cease the addiction.

Q: Is it necessary for me to eat organic food in order to control yeast overgrowth?

A: It would be better if you can, so that you will not introduce more chemicals (from chemical pesticides and fertilizers) into your body. However, if this is not feasible, regular produce is fine.

Q: Is it more expensive to stay on Dr. J's anti-yeast nutritional program than eat "regular" food?

A: No, it is not. When you are on Dr. J's anti-yeast nutritional program, you automatically cut out alot of junk food. Many of my clients reported savings on their food bills once they were on Dr. J's anti-yeast nutritional program. Besides, you also save on your medical bills and increase your productivity when you are healthy and energetic!

Q: Should I not get on Dr. J' anti-yeast nutritional program if I cannot be on it 100%?

A: You can be on Dr. J's anti-yeast nutritional program at any percentage. If you can be on the program 50%, you will get 50% of the benefits. That is better than 0%! Don't let the excuse of "either-or" stop you from making an effort. I have seen people waiting for the "perfect time" such as after the holidays or special occasions. However, the perfect time has not yet come and they are still suffering from yeast disorder symptoms year in and year out.

Q: Why don't you include nutritional analysis in your recipes?

A: This cookbook employs a common-sense approach. I do not want you to become a fanatic about calorie counting, nor do I want you to calculate the grams or ounces of protein, carbohydrates, vitamins and minerals you are ingesting for every meal. *We should eat to live, not live to eat!* If you just follow the general guidelines in **Part II: A Typical Day's Menu,** and adjust your food intake based on the needs of your body for each given day, you should be in good shape. *Learn to listen to your body, instead of your mind, when it comes time to eat!*

Q: I am confused because there are so many conflicting nutritional theories out there. What should I do?

A: Again, use the common-sense approach! If your health condition improves after you have been on Dr. J's anti-yeast nutritional program for a few weeks to a few months, you will know this program is helpful to you. If you have been on other nutritional programs which contain information conflicting with Dr. J's anti-yeast nutritional program, and you are reading this book, then obviously your health is still not in order. The nutritional programs you were on before may not have been complete. My suggestion is: try our program and then decide for yourself which one works best for you!

Part X

About the Author

About the Author

CURRICULUM VITAE
(Summary of Selected Professional Activities)

Name: **Juliet L. Tien, D. N. Sc., M. S. N., B. S. N., R. N., C. S.**
Mailing Address: 12021 Wilshire Blvd., Ste. 197
W. Los Angeles, CA 90025
Telephone: (818) 907-9363   Fax: (818) 907-9343   E-Mail: isi@pacificnet.net
California License Numbers: P188 & RN 252774

EDUCATION:

Doctorate in Nursing Science in Mental Health, Family Health and Psychogerontology, University of California, San Francisco, 1981.

Master's in Nursing Science (M. S. N.) in Psychiatric/Mental Health Nursing, Boston College, Massachusetts, 1973.

Bachelor in Nursing Science (B. S. N.) in Basic Nursing, National Taiwan University School of Nursing, 1970.

SPECIAL TRAINING AND CERTIFICATION:

- Hypnotherapy, Chinese Herbal Therapy, Nutritional Counseling and Acupressure
- State of California BRN Provider for Continuing Education Programs
- Nationally Certified Clinical Specialist (C. S.) in Psychiatric/Mental Health Nursing.

SPECIALTIES:

Counseling for Addiction Control, Pain Management, Post-traumatic Stress Disorder, Domestic Violence and Victims of Crime, Sexual Abuse/Harassment, Attention Deficit Disorder (ADD), Chronic Fatigue Syndrome (CFS), Hormonal Imbalance, Permanent Weight Control, and Relationships.

GRANTS AND AWARDS:

1984-87   Ethnic Mental Health Nurse Specialist Training Grant, National Institute of Mental Health (Grant #: 1 To 1 MH 18112).

1986   Minority Nursing Leadership Conference Grant, California Office of Statewide Health Planning and Development (Grant #: 85-G0054).

1984-85	Institute of American Culture Research Grant (Attitudes Toward Divorce and Divorce Adjustment among Asian Americans).
1983-85	UCLA Academic Senate Research Grant (Divorce Among Anglo and Asian Americans).
1982-83	UCLA Academic Senate Research Grant (Self-perceptions of Aging among Japanese Americans).
1981-82	UCLA Academic Senate Research Grant (A Cross-cultural Study on Self-perceptions of Aging and Associated Factors).
1979-81	Title II Traineeship Grant (Grant #: 2 All Nu00289-04).
1978-79	NIMH Traineeship Grant (Grant #: 5 To 3-MH13621-05).

PROFESSIONAL EXPERIENCE:

1996- Present	Cable Television Producer: "The Holistic Approach to Health and Success."
1996- Present	Motivational speaker at various institutions including Daniel Freeman Hospital and Medical Center at Inglewood and Marina del Rey, California.
1995- Present	Founding President, Infinite Success International (An International Network Marketing Company for Continuing Education programs and Chinese herbal products).
1989- Present	Founding President, Dr. J's Health Institute and Professional Weight Management Centers, Brentwood and Woodland Hills, California (Chinese herbal therapy, nutritional therapy, psychological counseling, hypnotherapy, acupressure, mental health consultation and continuing education (locally, nationally, and internationally).
1990	Consultant, Whittier Hospital and Medical Center, Cross-cultural Health Care, Whittier, California.
1987-1989	Founding President, The Institute of Holistic Health, Santa Monica, California.
1982-1987	Consultant, Sigma Theta Tau, Gamma Tau Chapter, Cultural Research, Los Angeles, California.
1981-87	Asst. Professor and Principal Investigator/Project Director, Ethnic Mental Health Nurse Specialist Program, UCLA School of Nursing, Los Angeles, California.
1982-84	Founding President, Chinese American Nurses Association, USA.
1982	Consultant, Formosan Hope Line, Rosemead, California.
1982	Consultant, Taiwan Provincial Kaohsiung Mental Hospital, Kaohsiung, Taiwan.
1981	Consultant, Kaohsiung Medical Center, School of Nursing, Kaohsiung, Taiwan.
1981	Consultant, The Taipei College of Nursing and Teaching Hospital, Taipei, Taiwan.
1981	Consultant, Hong Kong Politechs, Department of Social Services, Hong Kong.
1980	In-service Educator, Self-Help for the Elderly, San Francisco, California.

1968-80   Psychological counselor, staff nurse, nursing supervisor, Director of Nurses in various counseling centers, hospitals and long-term care facilities.

SELECTED PUBLICATIONS:

Tien, J. L., <u>Breaking the Yeast Curse: Food and Unconditional Love for Magic Healing</u>, Infinite Success International Publishing House, Las Vegas, NV, 1997.

Tien, J. L., <u>Being the Best You Can Be -- A Practical Guide for Harmony and Prosperity</u>, (a book and six cassette tapes), Infinite Success International Publishing House, Las Vegas, NV, 1996.

Tien, J. L., "Chinese Herbal Therapy for Pain Management." Paper presented at the American Academy of Pain Management Annual Convention, Dallas, Texas, September 15, 1995.

Tien, J. L., "Chinese Herbs -- How to Get the Best Results." <u>Whole Life Times</u>, Malibu, CA, November, 1994, p. 59.

Tien, J. L., "Understanding & Healing Your Pain -- Using a Non-intrusive, Non-drug Approach." <u>COSI - L.A. Community Magazine</u>, Los Angeles, CA, October, 1994, p. 20.

Tien, J. L., "Kids Who Can't Sit Still--Attention Deficit Disorder." <u>Whole Life Times</u>, Santa Monica, CA, October, 1993, p. 16.

Tien, J. L., "Body, Mind and Spirit Connection: Nursing Challenge for 1990's." Paper presented at the 20th Quadrennial International Congress of Nurses Conference, Madrid, Spain, June 24, 1993.

Tien, J. L., "Attention Deficit Disorder." <u>Daily News</u>, Los Angeles, CA, Monday, June 7, 1993, L. A. Life, p. 27.

Tien-Hyatt, J. L., "Conquer Stress -- And Find Peace in the New Year." <u>Whole Life Times</u>, Santa Monica, CA, January, 1993, p. 39.

Tien-Hyatt, J. L., "Weight Problems and Yeast Disorders." <u>Family Living</u>, Los Angeles, CA, July, 1992, p. 45.

Tien-Hyatt, J. L., "Are You Sick and Tired of Being Sick and Tired?" Los Angeles, CA, <u>Fraternal Order of Police Journal</u>, summer, 1992, pp. 47-49.

Tien-Hyatt, J. L., "Too Pooped to Pop -- Conquering Chronic Fatigue Syndrome." <u>Whole Life Times</u>, Santa Monica, CA, January, 1992, p. 15.

Tien-Hyatt, J. L., "Boost Your Immunity and Vitality." <u>Family Living</u>, Dec., 1991, p. 51.

Tien-Hyatt, J. L., "Candida: It Does Anything But Sweeten Your Life." <u>Whole Life Times</u>, Santa Monica, CA, July, 1991, p. 27.

Tien-Hyatt, J. L., "Manage Your Weight Effectively by Nourishing Your Body and Mind." <u>Family Living</u>, Los Angeles, CA, June, 1991, p. 60.

Tien-Hyatt, J. L., "Mental Health Considerations Across Cultures." Chapter in Varcarotis, E.N. (Ed.) <u>Foundations of Psychiatric Mental Health Nursing</u>, W.B. Saunders Co., 1990, pp. 65-82.

Tien-Hyatt, J. L., "Keying on the Unique Care Needs of Asian Clients," <u>Journal of Nursing and Health Care</u>, Vol. 8, No. 5, pp. 269-271, May, 1987 (Article).

Tien-Hyatt, J. L., "The Holistic Approach to Pain Management: A Preliminary Study." Paper presented at the 1987 Annual Sigma Theta Tau, Gamma Tau Research Conference, Duarte, California, March 20, 1987.

Tien-Hyatt, J. L., "Self-perceptions of Aging Across Cultures: Myth or Reality?" International Journal of Aging and Human Development, Vol. 24(2), 1986-87 (Research paper).

Tien-Hyatt, J. L., "Holistic Mental Health Nursing: Combining Psychological Counseling,, Acupressure and Hypnotherapy." Paper presented at the Third International Congress of Psychiatric Nursing, London, England, September 23, 1986.

Tien-Hyatt, J. L., "Leadership Qualities: Determinants of Positive Self-Image and Career Success for Minority Nursing Leadership: Past and Future, sponsored by the State of California, Office of Statewide Health Planning and Development, San Francisco, California, May 16, 1986.

Tien, J. L. and Johnson, H. L., "Black Mental Health Client's Preference for Therapists: A New Look at an Old Issue." International Journal of Social Psychiatry, Vol. 31, No. 4, pp. 258-266, Winter, 1985 (Research Paper).

Tien, J. L., "Divorce Adjustments Across Three Cultures: Implications for Preventive Mental Health." Paper presented at the 1985 Biennial World Federation for Mental Health Conference, Brighton, England, July 18, 1985.

Tien, J. L., "Home Remedies as Alternative Health Care: A Cross Culture Study." Paper presented at the 18th Quadrennial International Congress of Nurses Conference, Tel Aviv, Israel, June 19, 1985.

Tien, J. L., "Do Asians Need Less Medication? Issues in Clinical Assessment -- A Nursing Perspective." Journal of Psychosocial Nursing, Vol. 22, pp. 19-22, December, 1984 (Article).

Tien, J. L., "Toward a Theoretical Model for Cross-Cultural Studies of Aging." Abstract, the Proceedings of the 17th Annual Communicating Nursing Research Conference, May, 1984.

Tien, J. L., "Cultural Variation in Life Satisfaction for the Elderly: East and West." Abstract, The Gerontologist, Vol. 3, Special Issue, p. 296, October, 1983 (Research Report).

Tien, J. L., "Self-perceptions of Aging and Family Networks: A Cross Cultural Study." Abstract, Southwest Anthropological Association Program and Abstracts, p. 94, April, 1982 (Research Report).

Abu-Saad H., Kayser-Jones J. and Tien, J. L., "Asian-American Nursing Students in the United States." Journal of Nursing Education, Vol. 21, No. 7, pp. 11-15, September, 1982 (Research Paper).

Tien, J. L., "Surviving Graduate Nursing Programs in the United States -- A Personal Account." Journal of Nursing Education, Vol. 21, pp. 42-44, September, 1982 (Article).

PRESENTATIONS:

Since 1968, has made over 180 presentations in the area of cross-culture mental health, holistic health, yeast disorders, Chronic Fatigue Syndrome (CFS), permanent weight control, domestic violence and victims of crime, sexual harassment, Post-traumatic Stress Disorder, Attention Deficit Disorder (ADD), Chinese herbal therapy, natural remedies for diabetes, and holistic approach to pain management in local, national and international conferences.

THESIS AND DISSERTATION COMMITTEES:

Served as a chairperson or committee member on more than 15 Master Thesis or Doctoral Dissertation Committees at UCLA and other universities.

MEDIA APPEARANCES:

Since 1981, has appeared as a host or guest in over 300 radio talk shows or televised programs focusing on the holistic approach to health and success. Examples: from 1987 to 1994, the host of radio talk show on holistic health on KIEV, KFOX and KWNK. In 1994, interviewed on KFWB, KMAX and KMPC, Los Angeles, California regarding the holistic approach to earthquake flus and blues. In 1995, interviewed on KCTV, Santa Barbara, California regarding the holistic approach to health and success. Currently, a producer of cable television programs entitled, "The Holistic Approach to Health and Success." Since July 1996, has produced over 20 televised talks hows for Public Access programs.

HONORS:

1986	The Most Outstanding Professional of the Year, awarded by Chinese Joint Professionals.
1982 - Present	Member of Sigma Theta Tau, International Nursing Honor Society
1971	Youth Model, awarded by China Youth Corp.

Order Form

Books/Tapes/Products	Price	Quantity	Subtotal
Breaking the Yeast Curse: **Food and Unconditional Love** **for Magic Healing**	$ 17.99	_____	_____
Healthy and Tasty: **Dr. J's Anti-Yeast Cooking**	$ 9.99	_____	_____
Being the Best You Can Be: **A Practical Guide for Harmony** **and Prosperity (One work book** **plus six cassette tapes)**	$ 149.99	_____	_____
ISI Weight Control Program	$ 150.00	_____	_____
10-Minute Meditation Tape	$ 9.99	_____	_____

Tax (California Residents: 8.25%)   _____

Shipping and Handling   5 % with $5.00   _____
(Priority Mail)   minimum

Payment Methods:

_____   MasterCard or Visa   No. _____

            Cardholder: _____ Expiration: _____

_____   Cashier's check or money order

_____   Personal check (Books or products will be shipped when the check is cleared. $10
            charge for each returned check.)

***   If you pay by credit card, you may mail, fax (818-907-9343) or e-mail
(isi@pacificnet.net) your order. If you pay by check, please make checks payable and
mail to: **Dr. J's Health Institute, 12021 Wilshire Blvd., Ste. 197, W. Los Angeles, CA 90025**
*** For consultation (in person or phone) appointment, or for information on Dr. J's
       Anti-Yeast Therapy Training Program, please call: 818-907-9363 or 800-715-3053.

Ordered by:	Shipped to:
Name: _____	Name:_____
Address:_____	Address: _____
_____ Zip	_____ Zip
Tel: ( ) _____	Tel: ( ) _____
Fax: ( ) _____	Fax: ( ) _____
E-Mail: _____	E-Mail: _____

Order Form

Books/Tapes/Products	Price	Quantity	Subtotal
Breaking the Yeast Curse: *Food and Unconditional Love* *for Magic Healing*	$ 17.99	_____	_____
Healthy and Tasty: *Dr. J's Anti-Yeast Cooking*	$ 9.99	_____	_____
Being the Best You Can Be: *A Practical Guide for Harmony* *and Prosperity (One work book* *plus six cassette tapes)*	$ 149.99	_____	_____
ISI Weight Control Program	$ 150.00	_____	_____
10-Minute Meditation Tape	$ 9.99	_____	_____

Tax (California Residents: 8.25%)   _____

Shipping and Handling   5 % with $5.00   _____
(Priority Mail)   minimum

Payment Methods:

_____   MasterCard or Visa   No. _____

              Cardholder: _____ Expiration: _____

_____   Cashier's check or money order

_____   Personal check (Books or products will be shipped when the check is cleared. $10
              charge for each returned check.)

***   If you pay by credit card, you may mail, fax (818-907-9343) or e-mail
(isi@pacificnet.net) your order. If you pay by check, please make checks payable and
mail to: **Dr. J's Health Institute, 12021 Wilshire Blvd., Ste. 197, W. Los Angeles, CA 90025**
*** **For consultation (in person or phone) appointment, or for information on Dr. J's**
      Anti-Yeast Therapy Training Program, please call: 818-907-9363 or 800-715-3053.

Ordered by:	Shipped to:
Name: _____	Name: _____
Address: _____	Address: _____

_____
              Zip
	_____
	              Zip

Tel: ( ) _____	Tel: ( ) _____
Fax: ( ) _____	Fax: ( ) _____
E-Mail: _____	E-Mail: _____

Order Form

Books/Tapes/Products	Price	Quantity	Subtotal
Breaking the Yeast Curse: **Food and Unconditional Love** **for Magic Healing**	$ 17.99	_____	_____
Healthy and Tasty: **Dr. J's Anti-Yeast Cooking**	$ 9.99	_____	_____
Being the Best You Can Be: **A Practical Guide for Harmony** **and Prosperity (One work book** **plus six cassette tapes)**	$ 149.99	_____	_____
ISI Weight Control Program	$ 150.00	_____	_____
10-Minute Meditation Tape	$ 9.99	_____	_____

Tax (California Residents: 8.25%)   _____

Shipping and Handling   5 % with $5.00   _____
(Priority Mail)   minimum

Payment Methods:

_____ MasterCard or Visa   No. _____

           Cardholder: _____ Expiration: _____

_____ Cashier's check or money order

_____ Personal check (Books or products will be shipped when the check is cleared. $10
           charge for each returned check.)

***   If you pay by credit card, you may mail, fax (818-907-9343) or e-mail
(isi@pacificnet.net) your order. If you pay by check, please make checks payable and
mail to: **Dr. J's Health Institute, 12021 Wilshire Blvd., Ste. 197, W. Los Angeles, CA 90025**
*** **For consultation (in person or phone) appointment, or for information on Dr. J's**
     Anti-Yeast Therapy Training Program, please call: 818-907-9363 or 800-715-3053.

Ordered by:	Shipped to:
Name: _____	Name: _____
Address: _____	Address: _____
_____ Zip	_____ Zip
Tel: ( ) _____	Tel: ( ) _____
Fax: ( ) _____	Fax: ( ) _____
E-Mail: _____	E-Mail: _____